# GENERAL PERIODICITY

## Nature's Creative Dynamics

by

### August T. Jaccaci

# General Periodicity
## Nature's Creative Dynamics

Published by:

*f*iddlehead Publishing
P.O. Box 405
Scarborough, Maine 04074

Cover Design by:
Susan Gault

Library of Congress Catalog Card Number: 00-132308

ISBN: 0-9667120-1-3

Printed in the USA by
Morris Publishing
3212 East Highway 30 * Kearney, NE 68847 * 1-800 650-7888

# Dedication

I dedicate this offering of the discovery of general periodicity, nature's fractal pattern of transformative growth dynamics, to the life-long generosity of my parents, Thayer and Helen Jaccaci, and to the personal inspiration and encouragement of Stuart C. Dodd whose visionary scientific work was central to the founding of sociology, general systems theory and now general periodicity.

I was led to the work explained herein and mentored by my long-time genius friend Rendle Leathem. And, of course, the major discoveries of pattern that revealed general periodicity were made by my colleagues in creativity: George Land with his work he calls the "theory of transformation" and John A. Gowan with his fractal pattern offering he calls "organization of nature" found while working his way toward the ultimate patterns of grand unification. The depth and magnitude of their work and the personal courage of their offerings created the foundation and arch stones of general periodicity. Mine is a keystone and together our work is another beginning glimpse of the tree of natural order and knowledge whose leaves are infinite. The gratitude we share for each other is truly the joy of discovery.

I am also indebted to and grateful for the personal lessons and inspiration of the following profoundly successful pattern-seekers of the deep structure in nature: Christos Athans, Itzhak "Ben" Bentov, Dirk Bornhorst, Kenneth and Elise Boulding, Gil Burnett, R. Buckminster Fuller, Fred Glimp, William J.J. Gordon, John C. Gowan, Derald Langham, Rendle Leathem, Margaret Mead, and George Prince.

One of the best ways to advance an idea is to hold a party in its honor. The Creative Problem Solving Institute, (CPSI) annual meetings hosted by Sid and Bea Parnes and later with Bill Shephard, provided the setting for the beginning and subsequent search for natural creative order. And the early sharings at Rendle Leathem's CPSI gatherings of Bentov, Dodd, the Gowans, Land, Langham, myself and others were firmly, wisely and lovingly guided by Betty Cox, without whom our meetings would not have lasted long enough to yield anything but noise. She can rightly be called a mother of invention.

In the preparation of this book, I have been under the excellent guidance and editorial expertise of my wife Joanne with help from her daughter, Vicki Spear. And Sue Gault has provided her graphics, editorial advice and encouragement as always.

The printing and publishing of the book was made possible by the generous financial support of Richard Spady and his helpers at the Stuart C. Dodd Institute for Social Innovation in Seattle. The publishing of the book has been under the creative care of one of my favorite writers, Phil Candelmo of Fiddlehead Publishing

My deepest thanks to all of the above mentioned and to two more, St. Francis of Assisi and Jesus of Nazareth.

# Foreword

Much of my childhood and adolescence was spent staring at the sky, speculating about the universe and its countless secrets. My fascination was deep, exhilarating and at times deliciously painful because I knew that the stars and planets I viewed nightly would not yield their secrets to me. So the questioning became an end in itself, a titillating game I played with my psyche.

As I entered into the grown up world of work, marriage, and children, I forgot my early ponderings. They were set aside like the jump ropes, dolls and books of my childhood. I finished college, discovered a career I was passionate about and began the long trek to middle age. Divorced and responsible for two children, I didn't have the time or energy to dream.

Then, in 1995, I met Gus Jaccaci. Here was a man who read, thought, wrote and spoke about the very questions I had pondered so long ago. Through a miraculous happening we became a couple and I learned about the work which had absorbed him completely for the past thirty years. I found myself shivering with awe at the new ideas and insights I heard and read. This book describes the core of that work and the genesis of Gus' optimistic view of our planetary future.

*General Periodicity* is a brilliant and startling revelation of the fundamental workings of the universe. The importance of this book can not be fully understood unless you grasp that in its pages are the beginnings of all we know, the plan for growth and expansion of everything we are and have done, and the essence of why all this came to be. Read it with care, as you would fine poetry or messages from a great seer listening to the Creator of All That Is. These words are a prayer and a primer, a canon and a call.

I ask that you read with your heart and think with your soul. Suspend judgment and let these sacred truths wash over you and bring you new energy and hope. The future of all life depends on our conscious intentions to move with resonance and reverence both on our own planet and in the outer reaches of space. This book will support you in your journey.

Joanne Jaccaci

# Table of Contents

# Preface

From a search for the unity of knowledge akin to the earlier pursuit of natural history and philosophy and from work done in contemporary general systems theory and unified field theory toward a new cosmology of grand unification, I have found a new synthesis. Building on the work of George Land and John A. Gowan, I have discovered an all-pervasive repeated pattern of transformative growth, development, and evolution, a general periodicity in all matter and in all creative processes both physical and non-physical. This general periodicity is a universal formative internal and external dynamic. It reveals an always-repeated unalterable sequence of four stages of growth, each with a distinct creative dynamic. When the growth sequence is completed, it ends in a stage of transformation, forming a higher order unity of more complex capability of interaction internal to itself and external to the environment. This general periodicity is, therefore, the sequential dynamic process for all creation, learning, growth, development and evolution and all increases in order and influence. It is the map of all universal intention toward increasing order, life, and spiritual fulfillment. The discovered pattern of general periodicity is, not surprisingly, fractal in nature in that every creative stage contains within it the self-similar dynamic four sequential creative stages of which it is a part and each of those stages contains the same dynamic four stages ad infinitum. The repeating pattern and process of general periodicity is fractal in that it can and does generate both larger and smaller images and forms of itself as it progresses in time.

I have abstracted the pattern of creative stages into the form of a map called the METAMATRIX ®. The map depicts the four stages of dynamic formulation of order each containing the sequence of four stages within it yielding a sixteen square graphic tool for analyzing past and present and predicting and planning the future dynamics of any subject. Several subjects including human individual life and species life will be discussed using the METAMATRIX ® map format. (See Figure I-1.)

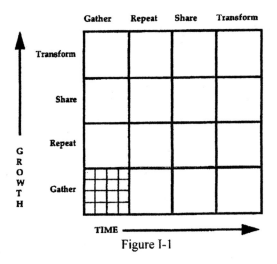

Figure I-1

Since all subjects enact the pattern and process of their general periodicity, they are all isomorphic, meaning they are identical in the structure of their dynamic process. In this way, for instance, the life of an individual human and the life of the human species are isomorphic and therefore, by their differences in development, they influence each other in a similar goal-seeking, reciprocal-causal way. They both cause each other to be becoming something new. Similarly, the external environment such as local ecology, human political economy, and conceptual cosmology are all isomorphic in their evolutionary dynamic and reciprocal-causal process, the nature of their influence depending on their respective stages and phases of development. In ideal circumstances, the more mature stages of being guide and facilitate the growth of the younger beings.

In recent human history, this guidance has not been the usual outcome, exemplified by a fully mature climax forest of redwoods enduring in perfect balance for thousands of years being destroyed in less than a decade by a two hundred-year-old human political economy. The same has been true for the destruction of human climax cultures. Conversely, compassionate successful evolutionary influence can be seen where the level of spiritual maturation of great individuals like Jesus and Buddha and Mohammed has inspired and advanced the maturation of the human species toward its own evolutionary fulfillment.

General periodicity can help us to design and orchestrate a higher order of harmonic unity and continuous fulfillment for all manner of being and for our human place in the whole family of being.

This book is written first in narrative form telling the story of the discovery of the universal pattern and process of general periodicity and then in analytical, expository and visionary form. The book is explicitly formatted in the stages of gather, repeat, share, and transform, which are the growth dynamics of the four stages of general periodicity. In terms of communication, the story of the discovery was gathered by individuals, repeated among groups and now seeks to be shared by the whole field of interested thinkers. The hope is that a transformation in consciousness will occur, recognizing and feeling the creative isomorphic and fractal order common to all known phenomena, lifting all life on Earth to a higher order unity and harmony.

# Chapter I

## Gathering the Patterns of General Periodicity

The story of the discovery of general periodicity began in the late sixties when I became fascinated with and began teaching the process of creativity. I was inspired and guided by William J.J. Gordon and George Prince to learn the Synectics process that they developed as a way to teach creativity. Then I was introduced by my friend, Rendle Leathem, to the newly emerging science of General Systems Theory and to the Creative Problem Solving Institute (CPSI) in Buffalo, New York. There, encouraged by Sid Parnes, the founder, and later by Bill Shephard, I helped Rendle form a study group to gather theorists whose work might offer contributions to a synthesis of general systemic principles. Our purpose at the outset was to educe a synthesis of theories to create the foundations for a new worldview.

On Deer Isle, on the coast of Maine, during the long summer vacations, I read about general systems theory and began observations of the profusion of vitality on the edges and boundaries of earth, sea and sky, systems so exciting, elegant and immediate to our shoreline cabin. And during those years, I remember praying to be shown the natural order of systems behavior.

With Rendle, we gathered a wonderful group of thinkers at CPSI, including Stuart Dodd, a founder of Sociology; Derald Langham, a plant geneticist and geometrician; Ben Bentov, a biomedical inventor and cosmologist; John C. Gowan, an educational psychologist; and George Land, the author of the transformation principle. Each man had a wealth of insight to share, yet Rendle and I were continuously frustrated that there was not interest in the synthesis of theories and principles among the participants. In fact, it took a strong woman, Betty Cox, using a three-minute egg timer to run our yearly June meetings and keep the contributions moving from person to person. After six years, the group dissolved, as we were not able to achieve the group creative dynamic of true sharing. Although we had met repeatedly, we came to realize that any work of synthesis would fall to the younger members: Gowan's son, John A. Gowan, Rendle and myself.

At one point a few years before his death, I was praising John C. Gowan for his work mapping the highest reaches of human experience and consciousness, and he thanked me and said that I should watch for the work of his son, which would be far greater in scope and importance. And with all due respect, he was right. For, John A. Gowan, completely self-motivated and privately working, was in pursuit of the completion of Einstein's search for a unified field theory, what today we have named grand unification theory, sometimes called the theory of everything. And with the prompting of the writing of Ken Wilber, John and I have known that such a theory would have to include not only physical phenomena but also the phenomena of the mental and spiritual realms.

Perhaps because of my interest in the nature of creativity and in the pursuit of general principles, much inspired by my work with R. Buckminster Fuller, I developed a profound respect for the principle of transformation proposed and developed by George Land in his teaching and in his book *Grow or Die.*

As proposed in the first edition of his book in 1973, George establishes that in the principle of transformation, the focal action is growth "defined as a process of joining in which ratios of interactive effect are continuously expressing higher levels of exchange...the process of growth continually transforms itself into ever higher levels of organization. The growth of atoms leads to molecules, molecules proceed to cells, cells join to become multicellular, and organisms recapitulate the growth processes at biological, psychological, and cultural levels. In every natural phenomenon there is the ubiquitous and irreversible procession from accretive to replicative to mutual growth, at which point, at a new level of organization, the process repeats itself." (Page 12, *Grow or Die*, 1973.)

This behavior or growth is presented in the form of a three stage standard "S" curve with growth on the vertical axis and the three sequential forms of accretive, replicative, and mutual growth on the horizontal time axis. Later, in a revised edition of *Grow or Die* in 1986, George renames his growth phases "forming, norming and integrating" to further emphasize "the very different kinds of growth typical to each phase." And he revises his "S" curve graphic chart to suggest a more correct theory and graphic. He states that, "no transition period exists between cycles; instead, one cycle actually overlaps another. A new phase one (formative phase) begins during phase three (mutual phase) of the previous cycle." (Preface to reissued 1986 edition *Grow or Die*, page x)

Although there is obvious and necessary truth in George's observation about overlap, it obscures an even more important fact that there is a fourth stage, a transition period or phase, which is transformation. Transformation is a moment in the growth process more distinctively unique and promising than all three of its preceding stages alone or in combination. After the third stage, integration, with its own internal formative activity, a new transformed identity emerges, so surprising and so capable in its new potential as to be usually totally unpredicted. That is transformation. And that is the transformation stage in which such things as a butterfly or a renaissance appear. Transformation is well beyond integration. It is the stuff of resurrection, the bringing back to order and life of a new higher order and new life. There cannot be a true transformation principle or theory without transformation itself; and that is one of the fundamental truths that revealed general periodicity, which made its discovery possible.

During these years, when George and I were using these concepts of developmental change in consulting work with educators and business leaders, and sometimes collaborating, I found it helpful to use more simple language about the growth stages. And, as mentioned, I found there needed to be a stage for transformation itself, the final outcome of a sequence of growth achieving usually unforeseen higher order identity, dynamics, and potential. So I changed the terms of the growth stage dynamics from accretive, replicative and mutualistic to gather, repeat, and share and I added transform. (GRST)

I defined gathering, saying it is the process of forming a sustainable physical being or idea. Growth is achieved through an increase in size and ability. The same being or idea becomes larger and stronger.

Repeating is the process of making multiple likenesses of a new being, product, or idea. Growth is achieved by the number of multiple likenesses repeated.

Sharing is the process of expanding by integrating differences and increasing relationships. This process creates a richness, complexity, and synergy from the union of differences that is greater than the sum of its parts.

Transforming is the process of creating a higher-order union of increased potential. That is, what had been a caterpillar becomes a butterfly. This process totally changes the identity of the being, product, idea, or relationship.

While I was applying these concepts in research and teaching in schools and businesses, unknown to me, another discovery of a different four-stage sequence of deep-structure change was emerging form the work of another member of our second-generation CPSI group.

What John A. Gowan did in his solo years of brilliant creative thinking about patterns of universal unity was to bring the ancient wisdom of astrology and the I Ching to bear on his deep understanding of contemporary nuclear and astrophysics. The integration of these seemingly distant opposite forms of insight yielded a transformation of astounding higher order unity and surprising unitive pattern: the foundation for general periodicity.

John discovered an archetypal pattern that repeats throughout nature from the formative photons to all evolved matter, to life, and to the galactic universe itself; from microphysical to biophysical to astrophysical. The pattern proceeds from a primal unit of action to a complementary pair phenomenon, on to a group or field phenomenon wherein lies an explicit 4x3 matrix of relational order, and finally on to an emergent compound new unit of higher order capability.

John showed us that for the universe to be born, unity had to achieve complementariness on its way to the multiplicity of matter. The unitive energetic form of light as particulate mass in time had to take on its fundamental pair complementary form of light as wave in space to thence move outward toward the break in pair-action symmetry, which allowed the manifestation of matter. The unitive gathering became wave repeating became the particulate fields and groupings that transformed intention, energy, and light into matter: our universe.

Also in this cosmic growth story, a dynamic is working in reverse to GRST, in TSRG order, supplying a force of great and primal attraction. A higher order transformed unity descends into multiple integrated photons of light which descend into complementary pair particle phenomena forming the atomic gathering process of creating the physical universe. This primal pattern of attraction will be discussed in the final section of the book.

John then made a chart of the repeated sequences laid out using the arbitrary attribute of size to depict the progression of order from photon to baryon to atoms to organic molecule; from DNA to cell to organism to species; from Earth to star to galaxy to universe. He called the one page chart "Organization of Nature" and put the four development lines each with the same four progressive stages in three levels of ever-larger organization. The pattern of unit, pair, group, and emergent compound new unit repeats throughout the three physical realms and levels. And in the first two levels, microphysical and biophysical, the emergent compound new unit becomes the formative unit for the next line of development. Here the size progression shows a developmental story which is a story of evolution itself from photons and atoms on to cells to humans and now to the emerging whole-life compound new unit of Earth Gaia, the planet as self-conscious evolutionary life unit. (See Figure I-2.)

### The Organization of Nature

| Creative Dynamic | Gather | Repeat | Share | Transform |
|---|---|---|---|---|
| Level | Unit | Pair | Group or field | Compound or new unit |
| **MICROPHYSICAL REALM** (Strong, electric, and weak forces. Four quantum numbers in three dimensions) | | | | |
| Particles | Photons | Particle/antiparticle | Three families of four particles; Three forces in four dimensions | Baryons; confinement by gluons |
| Atomic | Baryons | Electron-proton pairs Lepton pairs Quark pairs | Four quantim numbers x electrons, protons, and neutrons | Atoms; electron |
| Molecular | Atoms | Electron shell bonding; Inorganic molecules | Carbon: three Alphas of four nucleons; four valence electrons in third shell | Organic molecules and crystals |
| DNA | Organic molecules | Double helix; Base paring | Four bases of three chemical groups | DNA |
| **BIOPHYSICAL REALM** (Life force; four nucleotides code in triplets) | | | | |
| Cell | DNA | Replication | Genetic code; four bases code in triplets | Cell; membrane |
| Organism | Cell | Cell division | Three functions x four tissues | Organism; skin |
| Species | Organism | Sexual reproduction | Population structure x evolutionary fitness | Species; reproductive isolation |
| Gaia | Species | Speciation; hybrids and polyploids | Ecosystem homeostasis; four seasons of three months | Gaia; Earth life Atmosphere |
| **ASTROPHYSICAL REALM** (Gravitation; four third-order equations) | | | | |
| Star | Earth; Gaia | Earth-moon; gravitational orbits | Four x three gravitational field | Star; fusion |
| Galaxy | Star | Binary stars Earth-sun | Four spiral arms x three supernova generations | Galaxy: heavy elements |
| Universe | Galaxy | Andromeda Milky Way | Four dimensions x leptons, hadrons, and bosons | Universe; evolutionary time and space |
| First cause | Universe | Universe/anti-universe | Natural and divine law; four elements x three qualities | First cause; energy, conservation, information |

Figure I-2

When John presented his chart at CPSI, immediately I intuitively knew that there was an isomorphic relationship and creative connection between our two systems. They were in some way identical in the structure of their process of change, growth, and evolution. I suggested to John that transformation theory and four dynamic stages were the dynamics of the progression from the gathering unit, to the repeating pair, to the sharing group, to the transforming emergent new complex unit. We then added those transformation terms to a new co-created chart of Organization of Nature. (Figure I-2.)

We had discovered a pattern of the all-pervasive dynamics of developmental and evolutionary growth that showed that any and all increases in order of any kind at any level of time and size in the universe were identical in the structure of their staged process. For the first time ever, we had shown what adult humans know of their lives: that identifying the stage of maturity you are in allows you to predict the stages ahead of you and to care for those in the stages you have grown beyond. For the first time, we can confidently predict the future creative dynamics of anything when we have identified its place in its own story of growth and development. That power of prediction and wise stewarding of change and evolution were two of the surprising qualities revealed in general periodicity.

The final confirming discovery of the marvelous depth of general periodicity came the next year again at CPSI. John was giving a talk on our new Organization of Nature chart.

As he spoke and I listened with the chart in my hands, I made the same discovery that Dimitri Mendeleyev made with his development of the periodic table of chemical elements. One day, acting on an intuitive impulse, he walked 90 degrees around his array of cards in rows depicting the qualities of the known chemical elements. By doing so, Mendeleyev discovered order running vertically among the elements as well as horizontally. This discovery provided him with more information about each element, especially the three missing elements, which were soon discovered.

As John was speaking about our table of organization in nature arrayed on a single piece of paper, I turned the paper 90 degrees. In so doing, I discovered that the whole universe of order, the whole table from photon to the entire universe, was ordered in both directions with self-similar stages within stages. The whole universe of order on our chart is a gather, repeat, share, transform phenomenon with the same sequence of stages of order within order, exhibiting the fractal nature of elegant simplicity in the design and process of all transformative growth and evolution.

We then labeled the chart anew using the right-hand edge with the microphysical realm as the universe's gathering stage, the biophysical as the repeating stage, and the astrophysical as the sharing realm of the universe. The transforming stage, (not shown) is the metaphysical or non-manifest realm wherein lie the archetypal formative forces, patterns and processes that create the physical universe we know. The creative context of the transformative stage helps form the emergent compound new unit which is always the building block unit for the next line of four evolving ordered stages. And the new transformed unit has a rich crystalline magic. I have noticed that its profundity and potential is often the seat of breakthrough discovery that may then be the source of Nobel Prize recognition. The discovery of the crystalline, double-helix nature of DNA is a good example, as is the crystalline lattice structure of some matter, allowing superconductivity. (See Figure I-3.)

# The Organization of Nature

| Creative Dynamic | Gather | Repeat | Share | Transform | |
|---|---|---|---|---|---|
| Level | Unit | Pair | Group or field | Compound or new unit | |
| **MICROPHYSICAL REALM (Strong, electric, and weak forces. Four quantum numbers in three dimensions)** | | | | | |
| Particles | Photons | Particle/antiparticle | Three families of four particles; Three forces in four dimensions | Baryons; confinement by gluons | GATHER |
| Atomic | Baryons | Electron-proton pairs Lepton pairs Quark pairs | Four quantim numbers x electrons, protons, and neutrons | Atoms; electron | |
| Molecular | Atoms | Electron shell bonding; Inorganic molecules | Carbon: three Alphas of four nucleons; four valence electrons in third shell | Organic molecules and crystals | |
| DNA | Organic molecules | Double helix; Base paring | Four bases of three chemical groups | DNA | |
| **BIOPHYSICAL REALM (Life force; four nucleotides code in triplets)** | | | | | |
| Cell | DNA | Replication | Genetic code; four bases code in triplets | Cell; membrane | REPEAT |
| Organism | Cell | Cell division | Three functions x four tissues | Organism; skin | |
| Species | Organism | Sexual reproduction | Population structure x evolutionary fitness | Species; reproductive isolation | |
| Gaia | Species | Speciation; hybrids and polyploids | Ecosystem homeostasis; four seasons of three months | Gaia; Earth life Atmosphere | |
| **ASTROPHYSICAL REALM (Gravitation; four third-order equations)** | | | | | |
| Star | Earth; Gaia | Earth-moon; gravitational orbits | Four x three gravitational field | Star; fusion | |
| Galaxy | Star | Binary stars Earth-sun | Four spiral arms x three supernova generations | Galaxy: heavy elements | SHARE |
| Universe | Galaxy | Andromeda Milky Way | Four dimensions x leptons, hadrons, and bosons | Universe; evolutionary time and space | |
| First cause | Universe | Universe/anti-universe | Natural and divine law; four elements x three qualities | First cause; energy, conservation, information | |

Figure I-3

# Chapter II

## Repeating the Dynamics of General Periodicity

D uring the years of our first discovery of general periodicity when our ideas were jelling into final form, I felt that they could and should be abstracted into a generic thinking tool and creative process. As a painter, I had created a number of works that synthesized different evolutionary periods in time by overlaying imagery from each successive period. Sunlight, organic growth, industrial building forms, and electronic circuit patterns told a sequential story in one image. From this work and from an interest in sacred geometry, I created a map with a square made up of sixteen squares: the four stages GRST each with its own GRST internal stages. (see Figure II-1.) The resulting synthesis of ideas and patterns combines in one visual map the fractal growth so prevalent in nature with a rigorous process of human thought. As is right, people can not patent their discovery of general behavior in nature. Yet later I took the trouble to trademark the specific name of the map, META-

MATRIX ® because I felt the map needed a few years to stand in its precise integrity on its way to serving human thinking and planning.

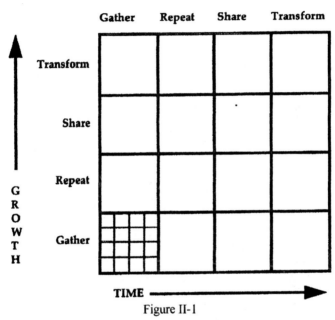

Figure II-1

The map reads from the lower left up each column. Each small square has its unique creative dynamic coded within it, starting with Gg, for gather-gather. It soon became obvious that each small square could also be depicted with all sixteen squares within it, as shown in the gather-gather stage of Figure II-1. Although the depiction would yield too much complexity at the outset, it does point to the beautiful elegance of nature's fractal process-pattern within process-pattern.

The potential use of the order within order in each small square is similar to the way even a small piece of a hologram can project and form the larger whole image of which it is a part. I decided to call the sixteen-square map the META-MATRIX ® because it depicts one over-arching metaview, a matrix of creative dynamic order within order applicable to any subject and story of growth and evolution. This application is true, according to the organization of nature chart from which it is derived, including the consideration of human life and on to the smallest things and actions we can discover.

To enhance the map further and show its own evolution as it is used, I placed the square map in a more organic context for its own potential motion of growth. I placed it in a golden rectangle. The golden rectangle and the spiral it generates are figures and patterns of archetypal growth in nature and in evolution. Therefore they make a good map pattern and process for any story of growth and evolution.

The golden rectangle has the golden mean proportion - 1.618 for the long sides and 1.0 for the short sides (See Figure II-2.).

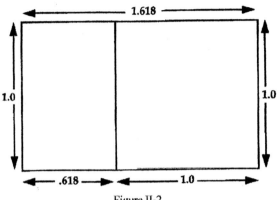

Figure II-2

If you remove the 1-by-1 square from the rectangle, the remaining piece is itself a golden rectangle in the same proportions as the larger one, as shown in Figure II-3. You can continue taking a square from each subsequent golden rectangle. The proportions of all these rectangles are identical. The diagonal line demonstrates the proportionality between two golden rectangles. You can also add a new square based

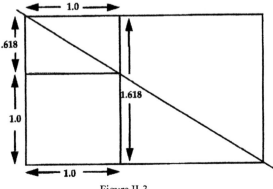

Figure II-3

on the long side of a golden rectangle, and the whole new shape becomes a larger golden rectangle. The edge of each progressive square used as a radius for a quarter-circle arc generates the curving archetypal growth spiral found in sunflowers, pine cones, seashells, the formation of a hurricane or spiral galaxy, and numerous other forms found in nature. This spiraling geometric pattern is itself an archetypal fractal progression called the *Fibonacci spiral* (See Figure II-4.).

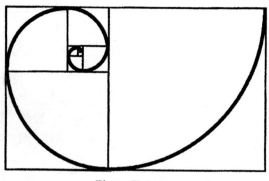

Figure II-4

With a sixteen-cell square nested in a golden rectangle and traversed by the archetypal growth spiral, I had created the METAMATRIX ® Map, a thinking tool for considering the past, present, and future of any subject as it increases in order and evolves. Because each of the sixteen squares has a totally different dynamic made of creative action, the differences help locate, describe, and predict the progressive stages of growth and evolution. Figure II-5 shows the METAMATRIX ® in a golden rectangle depicting a process-pattern of ongoing growth, learning and evolution.

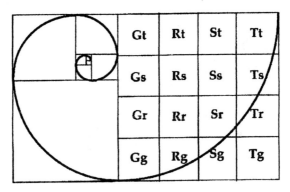

Figure II-5

As Gregory Bateson said, "Information is a difference which makes a difference." That is what makes the sixteen-stage sequence of different creative dynamics, from gather-gather (Gg) to transform-transform (Tt), a powerful thinking and framing system for analyzing the present stage of maturation and evolution of any growth process for any subject. Even more important, once anything is located in the sequence of growth stages, all its near-term and long-term future stages of dynamic, creative action and behavior are arrayed in front of it on the METAMATRIX ® Map. The map with the golden rectangle and spiral of the divine proportion suggests a thinking process that itself grows and reaches for its own future in an orderly way. As such, the METAMATRIX ® is an overarching, all-pervasive womb of natural order.

What the METAMATRIX ® Map does as one reads up each column starting at the bottom lower left gathering column with Gg and ending at the top of the right transforming column at Tt, is help the explorer find the place and creative dynamic of current growth behavior of whatever subject is being mapped. That placement in the sixteen square sequence then defines current behavior relative to success of growth stages completed and passages of maturation achieved to date and to potential creative stages of fulfillment achievable in the future. The map makes no specific future predictions, but it shows its power from its abstract nature. Each of the sixteen squares and their uniquely different dynamics of creative action suggest a progression of ordered organization ever more complex and capable in each new stage. The ability to consider the necessary unavoidable dynamics of future growth stages gives the user of the map stable sensible footing for creating conscious learning, growth, and evolution. Writ large, as we shall see, conscious human evolution now has a map formed and guided by general periodicity, the common way everything has emerged and evolved in the universe. It is a map of the series of exchanges which any subject or being when it emerges will and must experience.

When you discover that all being, physical and non-physical, follows the same formative sequence of g r s t, a strange and wondrous thing happens. You realize that there is no need for any subject or being to exist for the sequence of action and change to exist. That is, when any subject or being emerges, it will have to enact g r s t. In other words, this is how nature thinks without regard to the subjects that emerge to enact the sequence. The g r s t sequence of general periodicity exists as archetypal design before any manifestation at all occurs. And that leads us to believe that the birth of our universe has a prefigured story to tell, as does everything in the universe: everything, photons, atoms, galaxies, humans, ideas and civilizations, everything.

General periodicity is, therefore, one of the discoveries that will contribute to and be isomorphic with other aspects of an emergent humanly revealed grand unification theory of everything. In the history of planetary human civilization, this time with these ideas is the dawning of a global renaissance. The purpose in the archetypal story of general periodicity is beginning to reveal itself. Perhaps since the human being lies half way between the smallest things we know and the largest and is said to be half way between the apes and the angels, the human life story is where to look for that emerging universal purpose.

It is no accident that the archetypal image of the first human renaissance is Leonardo da Vinci's drawing of the measurement of man. Again, in the second renaissance, it is fitting that the life of humans be the measure of all things not because of our importance or threat to all life, but because we all have a life in common and it is this shared experience we know the most deeply and profoundly. If there is a grand unified reality we should be able to find it and know it in ourselves. As with the art of drawing the human figure, so well perfected by Leonardo, Michaelangelo, and other renaissance artists, when the body is drawn badly everyone knows it since everyone has a body. By the same token, all of us will know a good theory of human growth and development and future fulfillment because we are one. And we must come to agree on such a theory and become it if we are to rebirth and resurrect our unity with all there is in divine purpose.

# Chapter III

## Sharing and Integrating the Patterns of General Periodicity

Since we are of the universe and it is in us to the core, it is both fitting and satisfying to our natural curiosity to seek out the universe's patterns of omnipresent general periodicity in the human story. Our story, as individuals, is the one we know best. It is our measure of all things. The human body-based measurements of the inch, the foot, the yard and the mile prove that we can measure all things with ourselves as a reference. So in terms of the process of our growth, general periodicity offers us a new frame of reference to measure and chart ourselves and everything around us in a unified way. Yet this new measurement is not arbitrarily drawn from human life process, but is a universal dynamic which pre-dates all life itself. Therefore, finding it within our individual lives and within the life evolution of our human species gives us an elegant and powerful way to rethink the human story and tell it the way the universe and nature herself tell it.

One of the oldest intuitive questions and hypotheses is that human individual life repeats and relives human species life. That is often stated as ontogeny recapitulates phylogeny. Stephen Jay Gould in a book on that subject traces the history of the ontogeny phylogeny hypothesis showing that it was continually pursued too literally and therefore repeatedly proven untrue. Yet he ends his study proposing that in the future the common thread between individual humans and the human species may be found.

What earlier intuitive seekers could not perhaps see or imagine was that there would emerge a general periodicity of growth and evolution process within which all individuals and species are in fact simply unique and special cases all recapitulating a universally generic dynamic growth pattern. Since the general periodicity of growth stages is all-pervasive and therefore common to both, human ontogeny does recapitulate phylogeny and vice versa, phylogeny recapitulates ontogeny.

Once that ancient intuitive idea is found true at last, it can begin to serve as a guide and mentor for all groupings of human evolutionary life. The possibility of holistic conscious human evolution then becomes a working and workable idea. But unlike the established physical measurements, like the yard and the meter, the process of growth analysis and measurement is an evolving participatory collaboration for all of humanity. Because it belongs to and comes from within us all and is subject to constant revision and improvement, like world sports records, the following analysis, description, and synthesis of human ontogeny and phylogeny is perhaps a crudely drawn line in the earth. This thinking may signify a starting point for a new stage of the hopefully unending journey called human conscious evolution.

To more fully tell the human story we can take four leaves from the perennial book of philosophy. We can recombine the four branches of the tree of knowledge into one. We can make a synthesis of:

* *the physical, the body, the being of the universe: ontology;*

* *the mental, the mind, the knowing of the universe: epistemology;*

* *the emotional, the feeling and valuing of the universe: axiology;*

* *the spiritual, the heart, soul and spirit: the divine intention of the universe: theology.*

From the four perspectives of the physical, mental, relational and spiritual we can make a synthesis of the stories of individual human life development and human species evolution and of the inner being and outer works of those human stories. In so doing we are stretching our imaginations and concepts to make a union of in fact vastly different stories. But in that integration and union of differences and opposites, we create the context for transformation, for the surprising beginning of a new human renaissance and a new human fulfillment of divine inheritance.

Current discoveries in Africa of early human skeletons and footprints date a man and woman walking upright back 3.3 million years. In a cave in Sterkfontein, South Africa, a human skeleton that old is being slowly released from petrified earth and in East Africa male and female footprints walking together have been found of roughly the same age. That for the moment is the best evidence we have of the birth time of our species, of our walking upright. Studies have shown that the average baby will fall more than seventeen hundred times before learning to finally stand and walk upright. The whole skeleton of the human changes in the baby and the species when upright stance and walking begin. That is a fundamental doing, knowing, valuing and intending that defines and differentiates the human from others only one or two genes different from us such as chimpanzees.

At the time of early childhood our defining activity as hunters and gatherers begins. Every household with a young toddler knows the importance of keeping danger out of the reach of the newly free-ranging explorer with maximum curiosity and the eagerness to put everything in its mouth. Conversely, the early human survived precisely on the ability to range and travel freely and to follow where instinct, curiosity, and hunger led.

During the next years, spoken language also emerges and the inner mental life and the outer physical world begin a new relationship for the child and the species. The sense of membership and loyalty to family, clan and tribe emerges in the later years of childhood, and specific membership rituals emerge both in the child's family and the human species family tied to how these families live, protect and feed themselves.

Next, the more mature use of languages further differentiates families and clans and tribes. Among humans still hunting and gathering in remote areas of the world there is sometimes harmony but often competition and aggression for the lack of integration and positive synergy of differences. Territorial differences in childhood ego self-definition and in tribal hunting areas create more acutely important pressures in this time in the childhood of humans and humanity.

The pressure between the expanding inner searchings and increasing external territorial and cultural life combined only about ten thousand years ago to begin to transform hunting and gathering at some locations in the human species story. In terms of the METAMARIX ® Map of human growth, the many-million-year-story of gather-gather transformed to gather-repeat with the emergence of agriculture and the domestication of animals. The invention of that change ended the free ranging ritual of seasonal nomadic gathering. Now the planting of seeds and the raising of animals changed the human life dynamic totally to the gathering of repetition.

The individual human, having broken the bond of infancy with the earth, the mother, begins to bond to the rhythms and cycles of the larger family and families with whom it enacts its sustaining rituals. The new stage of being, knowing, feeling, valuing and intending of agricultural family and village life create a radical transformation.

Perhaps the most surprising emergence at this state is the drawing pictures of words and speech which we call writing, the repetition externally of inner knowing and concepts. Some posit that writing was born to record and report, to tell again the number and nature of agricultural product exchanges. The human and humans are transforming by learning to separate from personal immediacy with all life to engage in replicative abstractions of meaning. Early Childhood is in full sway.

Village life in the gather-repeat mode of planting and herding evolved extremely rapidly into the expansive sharing mode of the city, state and empire. The late childhood stage of gather-share we contemporary individuals now know as the time of beginning school and learning to share different methods and uses of reading, writing and counting. It is a time of growth dependent on the power of obedient socialization. And at the level of civilization that differentiation of skills and jobs, and social obedience, made possible by the replicative surety of gathered food wherein humans are totally obedient to a parental monarchy and ruling class, that is the archetypal behavior which built the world's city states and empires, dating back some five thousand years. The so-

cial inventions and the architecture of people like the Sume-
rians, Egyptians, Aztecs, Incas, Greeks and Romans speak of
the almost incredible power of collaborative, obedient social
creativity of whole cultures sharing their world views and
ways of being. Yet their frailty, their brilliant late childhood
parental dependency and vulnerability, and their simultane-
ous inevitable need to mature beyond monarchy and parental
paternal authoritarian political economy poise these empires
for extinction.

In the western world we see a time of transformation with
the fall of the Roman empire (and later its eastern counter-
parts) and the rise of the ascendancy of the individual soul in
Christianity, Buddhism, Islam and many of the world's other
religions. In the western world we called this era of human
evolutionary transformation, which was the human adolescence of our species, the Dark Ages. Adolescence is not by
nature dark, but it does involve an involuntary release of
former childhood behavior in order to assume acceptable,
replicable, contributing adult behavior. And the turbulence
that can ensue as the human body involuntarily matures into
the biological capability and necessity of sexual reproduction
is well known to adults as an often disturbing and surprising
time of transformation.

At the species level, the dark ages, the transformation of
the gathering childhood age of humanity in the western
world, took some 800 years to complete itself. And the nature of general periodicity tells us that at any moment of
transformation we can expect a dissolution that makes room

for a reconfiguration and formation of a new higher order unity of capability. The body of the caterpillar in its cocoon totally dissolves in order to reform itself into a butterfly able to break out and leave behind crawling for flying.

It is truly amazing how fast the general periodic evolution of the human species proceeded and accelerated from millennia to centuries to decades once the dynamic action of the sequential stages began their transformative changes. And it is equally amazing how much is lost from human life with the transformation to each new dynamic stage. Yet since the changes are inevitable and irreversible and are based on the carry-through capabilities from prior stages, we tend to focus on the most amazing story of all: the tremendous increase of power and evolutionary creativity in the nature of human life. However, in recent times we have had to question the amount of that power invested in the nurturance of human life and the resultant threat to all other life produced by human culture.

We were hunters and gatherers for nearly three and a half million years, utilizing extensions of our physical selves in evolving tools and shelters. Sufficient numbers of indigenous climax cultures made up of small bands and tribes of people still exist on the planet to enable us to understand the wonderful harmony and perfect balance these people have of all within them and around them. They live reverent, elegantly simple, totally self-sufficient lives in no way toxic to their surroundings and other forms of life. They are an ever more precious gift of exemplary living to us in the contemporary world culture ... if we can learn to accept and revere it. The Yanomami of the Venezuelan rain forest, the Aborigines of central Australia, the Eskimos and Lapps of the northern arctic regions, the Bushmen of Africa, the traditional Hopi of Arizona, all these are among the world's indigenous cultures which are all now under tremendous external pressures to change and assimilate into their surrounding dominant cultures at great and tragic loss to both. A fully mature, totally harmonious climax culture successfully balanced for thousand of years is like a climax forest or prairie or island chain. Climax cultures in their climax environments are critical lessons to us about the hows and the whys of future cultures on the planet. These questions of the meaning and method of life itself always come into acute awareness during the definitive stage of transformation. Adolescence is a transformation that acutely calls into consciousness the dynamics of replication, the biological and cultural repetition of life itself by the creative dynamic of multiple repetitions.

During the 800 years of the dark ages, the collapse of existing cultures, barbarism, murderous intolerance, and plague lived side by side with the emergence of geographical and natural exploration, cosmological and historical redefinition, and religious purification. And from this transformative cauldron of potential emerged a whole new general periodic dynamic as the foundation and founding of new higher order human life. With the necessary and evolutionary emergence from gathering to repeating, repetition became the organizing principle of human life. Therefore, we call this emergent era of young adult behavior the Renaissance - the rebirth, the repetition at this time of a conscious birth. The degree of acute consciousness of human life is so well depicted in Renaissance art which leaves behind its iconic former self to probe so deeply and carefully into the inner and surface reality of the human body. This same depth of consciousness and care is shown by the young adult father and mother as they procreate together the biological repetition of life in their children.

Perhaps the greatest and most powerful gathering of repetition, however, at the species evolutionary level was embodied in the birth and development of science - the great gift of the Renaissance. The scientific impulse had a long and illustrious history in many of the world's cultures before the European renaissance. But what made science flower into a species-wide joint venture of discovery at this time was the simple yet profound recognition and enhancement of the principle that science is first, last and always repetition, the gathering of the repeatable. Renaissance science taught us, not without some eventual arrogant disrespect for nature, that the enterprise rests on the discovery of the universe's repeating patterns and processes which can themselves be repeated by scientists and validated by visual and numerical means which are also mutually agreed upon as repeatable. Take away the gathering of repetition and you have no young adult procreation and no human evolutionary science of any kind as we have known it.

The emergence of the renaissance and then the scientific era spanned a time of less than four centuries before it too evolved into its own inevitable transform of the repeat-repeat stage of scientific industrial production and consumption. When the second young child is born to the young adult family, they have entered into their biological and cultural repeat-repeat stage of growth and development. And similarly, when the archetypal repeatable resources and machines are gathered to create an industrial process for mass-manufacturing products, the dynamic of creative repetition is ascendant and ultimately dominates all behind it from the growing and catching of food to the creation of clothing, housing, transportation and even warfare. What today we call the scientific industrial complex is so powerful as a form of worldwide creative dynamic behavior that it has determined and controlled a world political economy that every nation state must accommodate. And this repeat-repeat stage of humanity is only two hundred years old in its time of leadership and dominance. The industrialization of agriculture shows clearly how the evolutionary process absorbs and transforms all its former relations and relatives in the human story of continual accelerating change.

When the young family grows to the point where its children pass through their own adolescence and launch forth in their careers seeking to make a difference which makes a difference, then that family and its individual parents and children have transformed again and entered the new stage of repeat-share. They are all contributing to sharing differ-

ences of intention, ability, and creation with the wider environment and culture. And repeatedly sharing difference is
precisely the dynamic of the last and current stage of human
evolution we call the global era of information, communication and knowledge.

This last all-powerful stage emerged under the threatening pressure of World War II and is only a few years older
than fifty. Radar, sonar, television, computers, satellites, the
Internet, and a host of other electronic communication inventions have made us now a world village in real time. As
we have mentioned, Gregory Bateson said that information
can be defined as "a difference which makes a difference".
Knowledge is the integration of those differences, and wisdom is in part the integration of knowledge. The repeated
integration of differences, repeat-share is the fundamental
creative general periodic dynamic of our current era. And
our era has already begun its own transformation. We are
entering our own future now, a conscious transformation of
the scientific industrial communication era into a new conscious renaissance, a planetary emergence into higher order
unity.

The next developmental stage within ourselves as individuals in the world culture and within our species evolution
is the stage repeat-transform. The dynamics of repetition
which define and empower science, industry, and electronic
communication are beginning to give way and dissolve in
order to transform and rebirth at a higher evolutionary identity and capability. Unlike the first European renaissance,

our adolescence, this renaissance is global in scope, and, in the contemporary parlance of individual psychology, is our species' mid-life crisis affecting the health and future of all humans. Adolescence is an involuntary passage, a biologically unavoidable transformation. Mid-life transformation is, however, while in part biological necessity, primarily an opportunity for redefinition and conscious rededication to life itself. Mid-life crisis is a crisis of meaning and can only be successfully passed by a conscious and principled act of creation, a renaissance of higher value.

As revealed in the chart of Organization in Nature, in the whole macro-realm of the biophysical, life is the subject and growth by repetition is life's fundamental dynamic. Imagine then the depth of the crisis of meaning when we are involuntarily headed into a dissolution and release of life's repeating dynamic and being offered the chance to reformulate human life on the conscious principle of sharing and integrating any and all of the differences we are confronted with in the vast complexity around us. It is no wonder that issues like assisted suicide, toxic pollution, abortion, rain forest and species destruction, and genetic re-engineering are all so critical and threatening to us. They all represent a threat to life, as we know it. And if we cannot find the principles to rebirth life to a higher more secure level of realization and fulfillment, our crises will destroy life and us with it. Harkening back to the title of George Land's book, the challenge is always grow or die.

Meanwhile, as might be expected, the institution and enterprise of science itself is in mid-life crisis trying to transcend the inadequacies of rational thought, and challenged by the frontiers of the human mind and soul where the dynamics are not physical, not visible, not replicable and not within the realms of manipulation by light or electricity. It is not accidental that three major initiatives in the realms of contemporary science are pursuing the unknown under the names of catastrophe theory, chaos theory, and complexity theory. With all due respect to the brilliance and nobility of these efforts, in their logical and rational procedures they are in the state that T.S. Eliot used to define his poetry when he called it "an attack on the inarticulate with shabby materials." To move into the vast realms of the human mind and soul, known to be instantaneous throughout the universe, and ever-newly unique in their being, the scientific impulse and agreement and intention must be totally transformed to find a new identity and capability and a higher usefulness.

Just as the transformations of agriculture, science, and industry will follow us and serve us in the next stage of our personal and species future, our immediate future renaissance, so will the transformation of rational thought. Since we have reached the upper limit of rational thought, it will be subsumed and reconfigured in a higher whole-body-mind-soul intuition, a wordless experience of higher connectivity and synergetic integration of intending, knowing, feeling and it will become known and felt more as resonance and reverence. The unitive power of music has been calling us in this direction for ages, and is now the unquestionable single language of the human species.

One of the most amazing realizations revealed by the consideration of human development and species evolution in general periodic terms is the awesome acceleration of the duration of stages. Since the transformation in evolution from the beginning of agriculture to the present, each new stage and dynamic has been usually less than half the years in duration of its preceding stage: ten thousand years ago the gather-repeat of agriculture; less than five thousand years back the gather-share of the city, state, and empire; eight hundred years the gather-transform of the dark ages; four hundred for the repeat-gather of the renaissance and growth of science; two hundred for the repeat-repeat of industrialization; fifty for the current information and communication era.

Using these dynamics of the sixteen squares of the METAMATRIX ® Map, we have completed seven stages and have nine ahead of us. It may well be that the repeat-transform eighth stage, the global renaissance, will complete its conscious evolutionary redefinition of humanity in just a few decades. Since the human mind and soul are relatively timeless in their interactive dynamics, we are demonstrably at the fulcrum or balance point of human evolution. In 1999, nearly three thousand new books came into print with the word soul in their titles.

The mind and soul are by their operational nature where the physical, mental, emotional and spiritual expression of the human individual and species find their higher unity of being, meaning and purpose. Three ideas - unity, peace, and harmony - emerged continuously everywhere during the television coverage of the New Year's Eve we chose to celebrate as the beginning of the new millennium. These unifying concepts amid the shower of world music are another indication that we are doing the work of a new stage. We will undoubtedly look back on that twenty-four hours as the beginning moment of our repeat-transform stage and of the birth of the planetary renaissance.

The present and near-future stage of repeat-transform is just beginning to emerge. During this perhaps two-decade renaissance, the global political economy is reshaping itself around technologies that enhance real time communication, connectivity and relationship. The nature of those human relations are becoming ever more critical as their emotional and spiritual dynamics become the value determinants of individual and cultural well-being. The new coin of the world economic realm is the quality of creative synergy in the relations, in the integrations, in the sharings that define knowledge, power, profit and health. Therefore, the formative work of transformation means the conscious creation of ideal relationships; their synergy, their doing ever more with ever less, being a key measure of their value and general beneficence. The power of those relationships will come to own and dominate all former kinds of productive dynamics such as those that power agriculture and industry.

When one thinks of much contemporary farming practice, it is clear to see the sequence of stages roll over and dominate and control each other. The scientific era curved plow such as that designed by Thomas Jefferson sits beneath an industrial era huge diesel tractor, which is guided by computer and laser electronics which get their weather guidance on board from satellite surveillance, which gets its synthesis of predictive power from global systems modeling, and is guided and motivated by world market economic forecasts. This sequence of changing perspectives and operating dynamics permeates everything we do on earth and is relentless and unstoppable in its continuous revelation of emergent human creation.

What happens in a major stage of transformation and renaissance like ours now, however, is that for a short period of time we play with all kinds of new potentials, and briefly anything is possible. Transformation is time outside of time, a window on possibility during which ideas and ideals are the context and the content, the purpose and the process of the whole creative action dynamic. Manifestation and formation come at the end of the process. Discovering potential is the work of the hour. The highest ideals are in the end the most practical realities. Nature over time always and only produces ideal archetypes of everything in the universe. Every flower, every seashell, every butterfly, every galaxy is the ideal perfect enactment of its purpose. That is the challenge to the archetypal human in the flowering of a renaissance. The painters and the sculptors of the first renaissance labored brilliantly to give us the archetypal ideal humans. Now it is our turn again.

Now is the time for the predictive power of general periodicity to play its generous part in defining and forming the future ideal human. Granted everything that now flows from my pen is not *the* future truth; it is simply my future truth, the sharing of which is meant only to help open a rebirth of pure potential. These are the first ever moments in human evolutionary history in which everyone alive is now responsible for the conscious creative evolution of our species and all life on this planet.

We have refined our greed and arrogance and ignorance into tools and techniques of death-dealing so omnivorous that they leave no spot in the vast web of life secure from our incessant toxicity and destruction. Yet that behavior can cease in an instant; and I claim that the patterns of general periodicity applied to our species behavior predict that we will transform our killing into birthing and nurturing and stewarding of all life here on Earth and out into the cosmos.

During our global renaissance we will use our collaborative compassion and creative brilliance to envision and become a planetary political economy and unified community whose production of synergetic harmony will usher in a civilization of enduring peace with total life sufficiency and generativity. The general periodic creative dynamic which will make this possible and inevitable is sharing, integration, growth by the synthesis of differences and the union of opposites. As its name implies, the sharing dynamic is the transformation of competition into conscious, creative, compassionate collaboration. Collaboration transcends aggression and competition by consciously engaging with others in fair, reciprocal, and balanced co-creation and co-responsibility.

These dynamic changes of fundamental behavior often can be best and most easily understood by extending important subjects through a projection of their four g r s t stages. This process of describing the four stages draws our attention to the "S" sharing macro-stage now being imagined and envisioned for our near-term future in this new century.

On the following page is a chart (Figure III-1.), which suggests general periodic growth sequences in the four fundamental domains of philosophical discovery: ontology, physical being; epistemology, mental knowing; axiology, relational feeling and valuing; theology, spiritual intending and believing.

*August T. Jaccaci*

## Suggestions of General Periodic Growth Sequences

| | GATHER | REPEAT | SHARE | TRANSFORM |
|---|---|---|---|---|
| **Ontology:** | | | | |
| | Structure | Process | Synergy | Love |
| | Body | Mind | Heart & Soul | Spirit |
| | Physical | Mental | Relational | Spiritual |
| | Form | Flow | Function | Focus |
| **Epistemology:** | | | | |
| | Instinct | Reason | Intuition | Love |
| | Wonder | Word | Wisdom | Worship |
| | Data & Information | Knowledge | Intuition | Revelation |
| | Signal | Symbol | Soul | Source |
| **Axiology** | | | | |
| | Fecundity | Productivity | Connectivity | Unity |
| | Aggression | Competition | Collaboration | Love |
| | Autocracy | Democracy | Biocracy | Amocracy |
| | Providence | Power | Pleasure | Passion |
| **Theology:** | | | | |
| | There is God | God is there | God is in me/us | I am/We are God |
| | Father Mother God | Order | Grace | Union and Love |
| | Intention to secure Order and Grace | Intention to control Order and Grace | Intention to resonate and sustain Order and Grace | Intention to manifest Order and Grace |

**Figure III-1**

## Ontological Stages

Starting with the perspective of physical being, in philosophy the ontological, the conversation begins with gathering concepts of structure and form and mass and matter like the Platonic solids and the atomic weights of the chemical atoms that make up the elements of the periodic table. Then the repeating stage sees the advent of concepts of energy flow and process and the pair reality of the particle and wave identity of the same phenomenon and finally the pair-process equivalence of mass and energy in Einstein's famous $E=MC^2$.

We think of the great stone architectures of Stonehenge, the pyramids, the colosseum and the cathedrals as exemplary monuments to the gathering of matter and mass. And as we shift to repeatable process in more recent times, we think of the dynamic continuous flow of water, steam and electricity. The monuments to their harnessing, controlling and using their flow process and power are the great mills, dams, locomotives, and dynamos of the world.

Now we come to the next stage of human ontological discovery still unfolding among us. That is the group and field phenomenon of the sharing stage in which we now see an inextricable relation between the space and time dimensions of matter, the mass and energy dimensions of action, and the new information and intention dimensions of evolution. The integration of difference defines information and knowledge and the wisdom of intention. Today the unified field relating space-time, mass-energy, and information-intention describes a new working potential to understand the reality of the physical universe. To fulfill the current promise enfolded in physical reality we must integrate these multiple perspectives, which in their synergy provide the context for transformation.

In the near future the transformation stage of the physical and the ontological will reveal a higher order unity of multiple perspectives. The union of the shared and integrated three pairs: space-time, mass-energy, and information-intention creates a crystallization into unity of the mental, emotional and spiritual perspectives and forms of our current reality. The physical is one of the four roads to grand unification; and in the beginning and the end we do not do the physical; it does us.

## Epistemological Stages

Another philosophical perspective is the mental and epistemological road to the same unity. In the infancy of our knowing we may, alone and as a species, learn internally and instinctively from our senses gathering and working with physical signals, data, and information. Then we transform to the repeating of knowing where symbol and word enter the mental learning process and information culturally worthy of repeating becomes knowledge. The repeating of knowledge leads to the emergence of such operations as logic, reason and systemic modeling which are currently reaching their upper limits of usefulness and capability in human life and are now often better done by our symbol processing machines. Those computing and pattern recognition machines are currently freeing us to evolve again from within to explore our intuition as a higher way of knowing. We are using our whole body, whole mind, whole environment and whole world culture all in combination in real time as the sharing integration of how we know and communicate. This intuition is also accessing the wisdom of the heart leading to the increasing awareness of our soul. Thinking of, with, and for the soul creates the context for a future of revelation and illumination wherein human knowing transforms into cosmic consciousness. That consciousness transforms us into beings knowing the unity of the universe. In this grand moment of unity, we do not learn the universe, we simply know that it knows us, and we are it.

## Axiological Stages

Still another road to unity is the axiological, the valuing and feeling of reality.

Our life and lives may first feel and value the fecundity and nurturance of the mother and of the mother earth. The cry of the infant and the search of the hunter-gatherer seek to feed the hunger feelings of the body's needs. Axiological value often revolves around feeling the power of the parent or monarch ranging in behavior from predatory aggression to beneficence and nurturance and love. Children are dependent and at the mercy of their parents, subjects at the mercy of their king or queen or ruler. These are some of the relations that create the matrix of value and feeling in the gathering stage of development and evolution.

With adolescence and young adult behavior, we are guided both personally and politically by the feelings and values of independence. We move toward the formation of new identity, new family and new nations in the world community. The former power and authority of the parent and the ruler, autocracy, is transformed through the individual egoistic struggle and the wars of independence to become the power of the people, democracy.

As power is shared more widely, individual and group creativity in its profusion is measured by its productivity and multiplicity. Competition among and between the many repeated initiatives becomes itself a value with all its attendant feelings running the gamut from defensive fear to collaborative celebrative joy. However, there is a limit to the amount any environment can sustain predatory aggression or competition as chosen focal values. These are not the fundamental nature and enduring dynamics and values of life. Symbiosis is. Positive synergy is. Sharing is. Integration is. Life is a web of mutual nurturance. A great deal of predatory consumption goes on in nature yet that vital consuming is a balanced give and take agreement. By far the most energy is spent by all the members of the web contributing their gifts to the web and to each other. Life is synergy for the common good.

As humans, we have reached the environmental planetary upper limit of using aggressive competition as our multiple repetition dynamic and our independent productivity dynamic. The transformation of our values and feelings toward the creative collaborative compassion of sharing differences has begun, consciously, purposely.

While the feeling of the first two macro-stages of human evolution centered around pain and power, the transformation to sharing creates the emergence of pleasure as a central feeling and value dynamic. Not hedonism, but the fulfilling joy of giving the best of oneself to a higher purpose becomes the most valuable coin of the new sharing realm. Inasmuch as fecundity and productivity have been prior focal values, connectivity and the pleasure of a creative community are now the focus. While the prior stages centered on the feelings and values of the body and the mind, the heart and soul are now ascendent.

While the shift toward democracy is still emerging, a new form of political economic power is gathering its sharing dynamic at the level of the organization and the nation-state. The all-pervasive over-arching power of all life itself which I call Biocracy is appearing. As humanity is coming to realize that ultimately all life and all species must thrive and prosper or eventually none will, the values of dominance and control are giving way to the values and feelings of resonance and reverence.

Reverence, then, speaks of the fourth stage of human learning and concern, the transformation stage. In the sharing stage of integration and conscious relationships our values and feelings evolve toward ever more creative synergy and compassion. In the transform stage, we focus on and educe the feelings and values of the highest ideals to which we can aspire.

## Theological Stages

The aspirations and grounding of the human heart and soul, then, speak of the fourth philosophical perspective, the search for the divine and the first cause: theology. It is both an ancient and contemporary truth that the search to understand cosmic or divine intention and the first cause and unfolding manifestation of the universe create a natural union between theology and cosmology. This union of science and spirit is perfectly exemplified by the fact that the father of modern science and cosmology, Sir Isaac Newton, had an appointment as professor of mathematics at Cambridge when only 26 which found him as equally engaged in matters philosophical and theological as mathematical, physical, and cosmological. Newton's definition of God was over 800 words long. A close look at the life of Albert Einstein reveals the same comprehensive and compassionate interest in the intentions of the universe with respect to human spiritual and political peace.

Today, after more than three hundred years of scientific separation and absence from such comprehensive interest and synthesis of theory, a reconvergence of understanding of the actions and intentions of the universe is under way. A transformation is afoot to a higher order unity-primordial and eternal - long waiting to be discovered. Beyond and behind light, electricity, and gravity is love. The universe in its source, substance and future is love; it is made manifest from love, by love, of love and for love.

The cosmological reality of love has always been explained and prophesied by the great mystics, saints, seers, and holy ones. Now their prophecies are coming into present reality and the world is transcending former horror and suffering and pain to transform into unified harmony with all life by creating enduring regenerative peace.

The stages of general periodicity applied to the stages of human individual development and species evolution make this ideal intentional outcome not only believable but inevitable. The four perspectives of the philosophical description of our reality converge through the integration of their physical, mental, relational, and spiritual differences into their eternal unity as axial dimensions of one diamond crystal of love.

The theological-cosmological consideration of general periodic stages in all time dimensions of human growth is the fitting story of our transformation. The gathering of the physical, next the mental, and lastly the relational all together into the transformative spiritual once again enacts the gather, repeat, share, transform archetypal, generative, and universal sequence. The chart (Figure III-1.) is a preliminary sketch of developmental and evolutionary general periodic stages and sequences of growth. It is meant to be a beginning point of discussion and learning for our telling and becoming the human story of divine fulfillment. I will explore in depth a cosmology of love in another book to follow entitled: *Grand Unification: Future Love and Future Wisdom.* However, for the purpose of a short introduction to the emerging cosmology to conclude this book, here is a brief visionary consideration of the potential of our transformation reaching from the lives of individuals, to groups, to whole communities, to the entire human species.

# Chapter IV

## Transforming:  Future Love and Future Wisdom:
## The Dawn of Divine Reunion

Though it was inevitable, still it is truly amazing that the necessary wisdom within us and among us is evolving; that humanity is awakening to the realization that the universe is made of love, by love, for love.

Like the delightful surprise of meeting an old friend, a whole new unforeseen stage in our species evolution is upon us from within us. The realization about love is uniting humanity with all life in a new sanctuary of common understanding and behavior.  We are maturing into a global indigenous culture wherein all our endeavors are becoming one seamless web of sanctity.  It is a brilliant creative and sacred world culture unified for infinite diversity.  It bends in common action like all our human fingers, while it expresses infinitely different patterns like all our fingerprints.

For love is infinite in experience and meaning.  How could it not be?  It is the source substance and future of all being. So if we would build a culture, let us build it on a web of love and it will be both ephemeral and timeless, momentary and enduring.

The universe, born in a burst of light and sound, should have faded to silence and returned to darkness like a match in the night. But love broke the symmetry and light remained. Light carried love into matter in that first instant. Light is bound love. Matter is bound light. We are made of that gift of light from the first instant. The material substance of our bodies began at that birth moment of the universe. We are now entirely made of the primal intention and substance of the universe.

By the primordial principle of conservation that energy can neither be created nor destroyed, the break in symmetry became a debt to conservation and love. That debt took the form of gravity. The gravity which binds and forms the cosmos is matter's memory that it once was light. Gravity serves to hold the debt of broken symmetry so that light and matter may return to love from whence they came.

We too are love returning; we are returning life to love. And we are just now consciously awakening to that purpose, to our future love and future wisdom.

We have a new cosmology emerging, a new tool for understanding and using the workings of the universe. Cosmology, the study of the origin and order of the cosmos, has always given us our founding tools for the creation of civilizations. Newton's action-reaction cosmos gave us the science and industry which now both enhance and threaten life on Earth. Einstein's relativistic cosmos gave us atomic and light technologies, which now also enhance and absolutely threaten life on Earth. It is clear that we are the creators of our cosmologies and solely responsible for their intention and outcome. The universe is so vast it will answer any cosmological question we put to it. Newton asked: "What are the principles of motion and action?" Einstein asked: "What are the meanings of time and moving frames of reference?"

It is now time to ask the universe a new cosmological question: "What is love?"

No longer is it the job of one man alone to ask, but the job of all humanity. No one needs to be a physicist to ask about love, only a lover. And every man, woman, and child is a lover. Animals and all other life forms are lovers too. But they do not have cosmologies; they are cosmologies.

Thus humanity has arrived at the moment of creative responsibility. We are all awakening to a moment of conscious intentional relationship with the universe. Dominance and control of nature and the world environment is a stage of youthful assertiveness we are now transcending. Once again we are coming to understand that the world environment and the world economy are the same thing. Native cultures and farming cultures have always known this. But for a few hundred years, within the haze of the new process of industrialization, we have forgotten our small reverent part in the vast scheme of nature. It is now a source of illumination for us that the astronauts looking down on Earth or back at it from afar all fall in love with her each in their own way with their own reverent language which always transcends the manmade divisions and struggles that rack our lives down here on the surface. The astronauts are calling to humanity to join the family of life in a wider universe and to honor the beauty and sanctity of our home planet Earth.

Meanwhile there is an acceleration in human learning. We can feel it in our personal lives. There is a purification going on. Our intentions and actions and those of others are being ever more rapidly and openly understood by the world culture. This understanding frees us and helps us find and create more ideal intentions and behaviors.

To assist our learning, we have our whole species evolution past, present, and possible spread out around us in the settings and stories of the Earth. On almost every continent of the Earth all our stages of development are present. Native cultures live the lives of hunters and gatherers, which they have done since our beginnings tens of thousands of years ago. Farming cultures, our next evolutionary stage, emerged within the last ten thousand years. Science-based industrialized cultures evolved within the last two hundred years. And now electronic information and communication cultures that began only fifty years ago blanket the planet. Each new culture with its new cosmological dynamics and new tools gains power and control over all the earlier forms of culture. This sequence of dominance is inevitable, and as each shift occurs, we have been brutal to the older hunter, farmer, and factory worker members of our human family.

The geometric acceleration of cosmological and techno-logical change has become so visible that we have reached the point where we must take full conscious responsibility for creating our new cosmology and for the compassionate evolving of human culture and human life. That creative act of responsibility is happening now. This time is our awak-ening to the meaning of human life. It is our emergence into the planetary renaissance of our species.

Einstein's equation $E=MC^2$ establishes light as the natural harmonic frequency of the physical universe. We have built atomic, electronic and light technologies and a world culture of fear and hope on that universal truth. Now it is time to ask, "What is light?" and, "Why is light"? And what is our next cosmology and world culture? Will it be built on the invisible eternal truths whose realm is beyond the speed of light?

In numerous recent experiments it has been proven that while our brains work on electronic and light impulses, our minds are different. They are instantaneously everywhere in the universe wherever we direct them without the necessary traveling time of light and electricity. The human mind and soul live in the timeless eternal realm of the universe. And, while light is the natural frequency of the physical universe, love is the natural frequency of the timeless eternal universe.

Some people report seeing an idea flash over the top of a person's head as it goes from the timeless realm into the realm of physical visible behavior. This flash of light, in cosmic dimensions, is the same event that formed the physical universe. The idea of love changed realms and flashed into light and matter to form the universe. Love left the timeless, eternal realm of infinitely high vibration and slowed down to become the visible manifest realm of light and matter. A similar process occurs when high frequency inaudible radio waves are stepped down and slowed down through a crystal to form the waves that create and carry air-borne sound that we can hear from a radio. The process works to increase speed also. Slower sound waves can be traduced into radio waves that travel at the speed of light.

Now in the purification process going on throughout humanity our individual consciousness is being speeded up. It is an awakening of our body's natural frequency upward toward resonance with the universal frequency of love. As we purify our hearts and our intentions, our emotional, mental and spiritual consciousness is more free and open to vibrate at the higher frequency of love. That frequency of love is the source of life and permeates every cell in our bodies, but it takes a purifying and release of the lower rhythms and drum beats of meaning that detain us and control us to allow the higher harmonic of love to ring clear in our hearts, minds, and souls.

Meditation and prayer are two of the best ways to empty out the lower vibrations so that the primal grace of love in our beings can ring forth. Meditation and prayer are how the great spiritual leaders in our history have found the truths that help to inspire and guide us. And in this way, those in monastic and spiritually-centered lives have dedicated themselves to servant leadership for us. They are holding the future of our conscious wisdom. We now are beginning to understand that the benevolent use of spirit in our lives is the next stage of human evolution. Our entrance into that next stage of consciousness is the purpose of our newly forming cosmology and its complementary spiritual technologies. We are building the arch of human triumph. With a new sacred social architecture, we are creating a way to move into future love and future wisdom, our divine inheritance and our spiritual fulfillment.

# Bibliography

Ainsworth - Land, George, T. *Grow or Die*. New York: John Wiley and Sons, 1986.

Athans, Christos. *The Rainbow Theory of Economics*. In process.

Bentov, Itzhak. *Stalking the Wild Pendulum*. Rochester, Vt.: Destiny Books, 1988.

Boulding, Elise. *Building a Global Civic Culture: Education for an Interdependent World*. Teachers College Press, 1988.

Boulding, Kenneth. *Ecodynamics: A New Theory of Societal Evolution*. Sage Publications, 1978.

Clark, Kenneth. *Leonardo da Vinci*. London: Penguin Books, 1989.

Dodd, Stuart C. *Probable Acts of Men*, two volumes. State University of Iowa, 1963.

Eliot, T.S. *On Poetry and Poets* (essays). Farrar, Straus, 1957.

Fuller, R. Buckminster. *Critical Path*. New York: St. Martin's Press, 1981.

# Bibliography

Gordon, William J.J. *Synectics*. Harper Row, 1961.

Gould, Stephen Jay. *Ontogeny and Phylogeny*. Belknap Press, 1977.

Gowan, John A. and August T. Jaccaci. *Grand Unification*. Portland, Maine: Unity Scholars.

Gowan, John C. *Trance Art and Creativity*. Buffalo, NY: Creative Education Foundation, 1975.

Jaccaci, August T. and Susan B. Gault. *CEO: Chief Evolutionary Officer*. Boston: Butterworth-Heinemann, 1999.

Jefferson, Thomas. *Notes on the State of Virginia*. Viking Press, 1998.

Kelman, Peter. *Mendeleyev: Prophet of Chemical Elements*. Englewood Cliffs, NJ: Prentice Hall, 1970.

Land, George T. Lock. *Grow or Die*. New York: Random House, 1973.

Land, George and Beth Jarman. *Breakpoint and Beyond*. New York: Harper Business, 1992.

# Bibliography

Langham, Derald. *Genesa*. Fallbrook, CA: Aero Publishers, 1969.

Mead, Margaret. *World Enough: Rethinking the Future.* Little Brown, 1975.

Nathan, Otto and Heinz Norden, editors, preface by Bertrand Russell. *Einstein on Peace.* Simon and Schuster, 1960.

Newton, Isaac. *Mathematical Principles of Natural Philosophy.* Chicago: Encyclopedia Brittanica, 1952.

Parnes, Sidney J. *The Magic of Your Mind.* Bearly Limited, 1981.

Prince, George. *The Practice of Creativity.* New York: Collier Books, 1972.

Spady, Richard J. and Cecil H. Bell, Jr. *The Business of Civilization Building: Administrative Theory and Citizen Skills for the 21$^{st}$ Century.* In process.

Wilber, Ken. *A Brief History of Everything.* Boston: Shambala, 1996.

# Index

# Index

# Index

# Index

# Index

## Book Orders

Orders for additional books may be addressed to:

Unity Scholars
45 High Bluff Road
Cape Elizabeth, Maine 04107

or to order autographed copies and for more information
about available workshops and speeches,
please contact the author:

August Jaccaci
45 High Bluff Road
Cape Elizabeth, ME  04107
e-mail:  joannegus@msn.com

Cost of the book from either source (including shipping) is
$15.00 U.S.